Thomas Nicholson

Nicholson's Roller Skating Rink Book

Containing over sixty Choice and Novel Attractions with full Instructions to

Rink Managers

Thomas Nicholson

Nicholson's Roller Skating Rink Book
Containing over sixty Choice and Novel Attractions with full Instructions to Rink Managers

ISBN/EAN: 9783337046903

Printed in Europe, USA, Canada, Australia, Japan

Cover: Foto ©Lupo / pixelio.de

More available books at **www.hansebooks.com**

NICHOLSON'S

ROLLER SKATING

RINK BOOK

CONTAINING

OVER SIXTY CHOICE AND NOVEL ATTRACTIONS

WITH

FULL INSTRUCTIONS TO RINK MANAGERS.

BY

THOMAS NICHOLSON.

PUBLISHED BY
NICHOLSON & BRO.,
RICHMOND, IND.
1886.

INTRODUCTORY.

In the preparation of "RINK ATTRACTIONS," the author indulges the hope that, by consulting them, managers of rinks may be relieved of much embarrassment in providing amusements for their patrons. While roller-skating is a delightful and healthful exercise, and entertaining to those who skate, it soon becomes monotonous to the spectators, unless there shall be some diversion aside from plain roller-skating. It is for the entertainment of this class of patrons, and they form a considerable quantity in the general attendance, that led to the compilation of the amusements herein contained.

We confidently believe that every manager will be amply repaid the price of the book, by the introduction of these attractions into his rink, in the increased attendance they will command. It has been the design of the author to add new features to old attractions, as well as to give many that are entirely new.

The long and successful experience of the author in the management of one of the largest and finest rinks in the country, will, we trust, be appreciated by those who desire to make their rinks deservedly popular.

RINK ATTRACTIONS.

---··o◊o··---

THE MAY POLE.

Place the pole in the center of the rink, and let it be long enough to extend from the floor to the ceiling, fastening it to the floor by boring a half-inch hole in the floor and inserting a peg in the center of the bottom part of the pole, and then set the peg in the hole. This arrangement will keep the May Pole firmly in position. To the top part of the pole eight, ten, or twelve ribbons are fastened, each ribbon being one-third longer than the pole, and each having a loop at the lower end. These ribbons should be about three inches and a half wide, and of red, white and blue color. The ribbons should be pinned up to the pole before the skating begins, in order to prevent them from getting soiled by lying on the floor. Describe a circle around the May Pole on the floor in black, the circle extending as far from the May Pole as the entire length of each ribbon will admit; then locate as many stations along the circle as there are persons to take part in the May Pole. Locate the stations equidistant from each other, and designate them by means of semi-circles, those for the gentlemen resting on the outside of the main circle, and those for the ladies resting on the inside of the main circle, and number the stations consecutively so that each person will know his or her station. At the sound of the gong or bell the floor should be cleared of skaters, and while this is being done the manager should go to the May Pole and unloosen the ribbons and place the end of each at its proper station, being careful that the ribbons do not get twisted or in any way any one interfering with the other. At a given signal the music, which should be a slow waltz time, begins, and immediately the skaters start from their respective dressing rooms, skating once about the rink in couples, headed by the leader, and followed in such order that they will come in regular order at the several stations about the May Pole. After skating once about the rink, skate to the circle, leaving the ladies at their respective stations, and the gentlemen remaining near them. At a given signal from the leader each gentleman picks up his partner's ribbon and hands it to her, then skates to his own station, and then all gentlemen at the same time pick up their own ribbons, facing partners; at a signal they all form the grand chain, the ladies going to the left and the gentlemen to the right, each gentleman skating underneath his partner's ribbon, then outside the next lady, and so on, the ladies observing the same movements in the opposite direction, all being careful to maintain equal distances apart, continuing until the ribbons are braided about the pole to a point about seven feet from the floor. In the foregoing movements the ladies should hold the ribbon in their left hands, and the gentlemen hold their ribbons in their right hands.

Just prior to the completion of the braiding the manager should indicate the same by two sounds of a whistle just as partners are passing each other for the last time, in order that they may stop and partners be facing each other. At a given signal all turn half round, changing the ribbons to the other hand, and reverse the movement, the gentlemen skating outside of the lady facing him, and underneath the next ribbon, and so on, until the braiding is about half undone, then stop as before directed, with your partner at your side and all facing the pole; then all skate to the pole and drop the ribbons; then skate to the dressing room in couples.

No one should be permitted to take part in the May Pole unless he or she can skate skillfully both to the right and left. The May Pole should be practiced several times before attempting to give it to an audience. The effect is made more beautiful by the ladies being dressed in white, and the gentlemen in conventional black or dark colors.

ORANGE RACE.

There should not be more than four contestants in this race. Place in the center of the rink a box containing oranges. At a given signal the contestants should all start together from a given point, and skate to the box, take one orange from the box, then skate to the limit of the rink on the right and skate on around the rink to the place of beginning, but without stopping, and proceeding as before. The participants are all to wear aprons, and they must hold the oranges in the apron. They are to be permitted to take only one orange at a time out of the box, and in case any one should drop an orange from his apron in the course of his skating, he must not stop for it, but go right on; but when he gets to the box he shall not take out another orange, but skate to the one he dropped and pick it up. The time should be limited to ten laps, and each participant should be allowed to keep the oranges he gets from the box in the race.

The excitement may be increased by giving a special prize to the winner. Where oranges can not be procured, apples will do as well. Appoint judges to decide all points, and thus relieve yourself of possible blame because of any apparently unjust decisions.

FOX DRIVE.

If a fox can be procured, this attraction can be made extremely exciting. Before the evening for the drive the fox should be turned loose in the rink, and run about by a half dozen boys, so that the fox may become accustomed to the place. If this is not done, it is possible he would become stupefied with fear on the night of the Drive, and refuse to run at all, and thus render the Drive a failure, and a matter of regret to the Manager. Woven wire should be stretched about the rink so that the fox can not get to the audience. When all ready, turn two young men into the enclosure, and then turn the fox loose. If they fail to catch the fox in two minutes, let two other contestants try it for same time, and if they fail, still two oth- other; and if they fail, then let all six try it, and if they are unable to catch the fox, the Manager will have provided a great deal of amusement with- out the expense of paying for the stipulated prize.

COUPLE RACE.

This race should be engaged in by three couples skating hand in hand, and not to exceed ten laps. Each couple should have a distinct starting point, and thus avoid a bungling start.

Racing in which ladies indulge does not generally meet with popular favor, and it is well to have as little of it as possible. It was this feature of the rinks that called forth such vigorous attacks from the ministry last season. Every Manager will have to be the judge of his own community in this respect.

RING TOURNAMENT.

There should be four contestants in the tournament. The rings should be arranged in sets of four each abreast, and suspended from the ceiling to a point about a foot beyond the height of the contestants. The sets of rings should be hung about twenty feet apart, and the number of sets will depend upon the size of the rink. The contestants are to start from a given point, each provided with a stick six feet long and one inch in diameter, and this is to be carried under the right arm, and guided only by the right hand. The rings should be of wire, and about two inches and a half in diameter. The point of the Tournament is to see who can thread the greatest number of rings on the sticks in a given number of laps. The rings should be suspended from the ceiling so that they can be easily slipped on the sticks, and yet sufficiently stable in their positions so that a mere touch of them would not set them to swinging. The better way will be to have them resting on a slight curve at the lower end of a stiff wire attached to the ceiling.

HAT NIGHT.

The night for this attraction should be thoroughly advertised as "The Hat Night," and all gentlemen invited to participate. There should be four prizes given. The first to the person wearing the largest hat, the second prize to the gentleman wearing the next largest, and so on. In the distribution of prizes they should be given to the persons actually wearing the largest hats. There will be apt to be a disposition on the part of boys to wear "something" of immense proportions without regard to its resemblance to a hat.

Where there is a general participation this attraction can be made very interesting.

TEETER-TOTTER CONTEST.

There should be four contestants in this race. The Teeter-Totter is made of a piece of two-inch plank, four feet long and fourteen inches wide, nailed securely to the edge of a piece of plank fourteen inches long and a foot high. The four foot plank should be nailed to the piece of upright plank just beyond the central point, so that one end of the four foot plank will rest on the floor, and the other end be elevated accordingly. There should be one Teeter-Totter for each contestant, and all placed abreast, yet not so near each other that one contestant would interfere with the other when they are attempting to go over them. The number of Teeter-Totters to be used will depend upon the size of the rink.

The Teeter-Totters are to be placed with the part elevated facing the contestants. At a given signal they all start, and each one is obliged to skate to the Teeter-Totter, and to skate over it, and not step over. The Teeter-Totters should be placed in rows at a sufficient distance apart, and the race should be limited to eight laps.

BICYCLE AND SKATE RACE.

When this race is contested by skillful partici-pants it is beautiful and exciting. Ordinarily a good rider will make a mile and a fifth, to a mile by a swift skater. The race should be contested with this proportionate rate of speed in view, so that there will be no favoritism.

THE NECKTIE CARNIVAL.

This Carnival is for gentlemen only, and is conducted just the same as the Hat Night Carnival. In instructing judges, have them observe that the Necktie must be self supporting, and look like a tie.

MEAL RACE.

In this race the contestants are required to carry a twenty-five pound sack of meal in such way that it does not touch the body. If the sack should be dropped or knocked from the hands of the contestant he is required to stop and pick it up before proceeding any further. This race will develop endurance and strength rather than fleetness, and should be limited to a mile. Sacks should be made of cloth, for if they are made of paper they are liable to burst if dropped.

PIG CATCH.

Select for this attraction a pig weighing about one hundred pounds, but not so fat as to render him clumsy. Chase him around the rink five or six times of evenings after the rink closes, so that he may become accustomed to the floor and the lights. On the night for the Catch have the pig clipped and greased, and then turn him in the rink. Only two young men should be allowed to attempt to catch him at a chase. It should be stipulated in the "Catch" that when one contestant has hold of the pig that the other must stand aside until he either gets the pig in the basket which should be provided for him, at the judges' feet, or gets away. A chase should be timed to two minutes. If the young men fail in this time to catch the pig, then two others try, and if they fail, two others; and if the six fail, then let all try. The pig is to be caught and carried to the basket, and laid in, and not thrown in.

This attraction is very amusing, and will no doubt call for repetitions. Be sure and get a wild pig, and accustom him to the surroundings before the Catch. This attraction was presented at the Main Street Rink, this city, last winter, and it drew over a two hundred dollar house.

COLLAR CARNIVAL.

This Carnival is conducted just as the other Carnivals mentioned in the preceding pages. The prizes should be awarded to those having the largest and best proportioned collars, which may be of any style, either standing or lay down. About twenty-five tickets for voting purposes should be distributed among persons who would be well qualified to judge as to who deserved the prizes.

HISTORICAL CARNIVAL.

This is an attraction that will draw a class of patrons that nothing else would, because it will be of necessity instructive. There should be a representative of each distinctive type of historical personages, and prior to the evening for this attraction it would be well for the Manager to ascertain just what personages are to be represented, so that he may be able to diversify them by not having two representations of one character. There should be representations of Kings and Queens of different countries, each in proper dress; of English and American authors; of famous actors and actresses; of men who have achieved renown in military capacity; of eminent journalists; of philosophers; of celebrated musicians; of statesmen; of lecturers, and any other historical celebrity. The person representing any character should acquaint him or herself with the history of such character, so that the representation may be as natural as possible.

It will take considerable time, study and preparation for this carnival, but it will draw an appreciative audience. There should be a liberal distribution of prizes, and judges selected who would be fully competent to decide upon the respective merits of the contestants.

FLOWER CARNIVAL.

This attraction can be made perfectly beautiful. None but natural flowers are to be used. There should be prizes for the largest bouquet and also for the smallest. Symmetry of proportions, variety and color of flowers to be considered. Ladies and gentlemen should both contest for prizes on bouquets. There should be awards for the most beautiful floral trimmings on dresses, and for floral decorations in the hair of the ladies, and the best representation of a flower girl. This is a beautiful attraction for children. Managers may sell enough button-hole bouquets to defray the expense of prizes.

KAZOO RACE.

Suspend four Kazoos from the ceiling by attaching them to strings, placing them abreast and two feet apart; then in same manner four small tin horns as far from the Kazoos as the size of the rink will admit, having two sets of Kazoos and two sets of horns.   'At a given signal the contestants start from a certain point.   The provisions of the race are, that each contestant shall be obliged to blow each Kazoo and horn in making the rounds without the aid of the hands; the number of rounds to be made can be decided by the Manager.   Judges should be stationed at the Kazoos and horns to see that none pass without first blowing them.   The contortions of the face that the various contestants will make in their attempts to secure the Kazoos and horns so that they may blow them, will be quite laughable.

OLD FOLKS CARNIVAL.

This, like the Historical Carnival, is for both ladies and gentlemen.   Prizes are to be given to the best representation of an old man, an old woman, and an old couple, of whatever nationality.   The manager should arrange so that there may be as general a representation of characters as possible. There should be American, Irish, German, French and Negro representatives.   Make liberal prizes,

and have the attraction well in hand before its pre-
sentation.

––––––––

BACKWARD RACE.

This race should not be contested for more than
a half mile, and the contestants should be obliged
to keep within bounds of circle described about the
Rink. The contestants are to start from a given
place and from a standing position at the word
" go." Judges should be stationed at each cor-
ner, to see that each keeps within the circle. It is
difficult to skate backward and keep within the
track.

––––––––

NATIONAL CARNIVAL.

This attraction can be made very interesting
and instructive. Have representations of all the
leading nations, with the characteristics of each
nation fully delineated. Arrange beforehand to
secure as diverse representation as possible.

CALICO CARNIVAL.

Both ladies and gentlemen may participate. Ladies should be in full calico dress, and gentlemen wear at least calico neckties. There should be a suitable number of prizes awarded, so as to make the attraction generally participated in.

REVERSE RACE.

This race is to be made with the skaters going in the opposite direction usually followed by all skaters. It will be difficult to turn the corners rapidly, and will develop considerable awkwardness that will prove amusing.

GARDEN PARTY.

In this attraction all ladies are dressed in white, and wear light hats; gentlemen wear white vests and white ties. No lady or gentleman should be permitted to appear on the floor unless attired as above, until after a certain hour. Prizes should be offered for the prettiest dress, and handsome hat, and for the gentleman making the best appearance on the floor.

A few tables should be placed in the center of the rink, upon which should be placed plants. Place chairs about the tables so that the skaters may rest themselves. This feature will make the attraction more realistic.

BELL RACE.

Suspend several single bells from the ceiling until they come within six feet of the floor. Station a judge at each bell. The contestants start from a given point at a given signal. Each contestant is obliged to ring each bell, and is not allowed to pass from one bell until he shall have first rung it. After ringing a bell the contestant should give it a toss in the air, as this will make it more difficult for those following to secure it. At one end of the rink should be placed a barrel within a circle drawn about it, and which should be two feet more in diameter than the barrel. In the bottom of the barrel put a cow bell. Each contestant should be obliged also to stop at the barrel and ring the cow bell. If he should move the barrel outside of the circle about it, he must place the barrel in its original position before going to the next bell.

SKATER AGAINST WALKER.

This race usually develops a great deal of excitement and interest. The proportionate rate of speed should be one mile for the skater, and three-quarters of a mile for the pedestrian.

FAT MEN'S RACE.

The fattest, largest, and clumsiest men should be selected for this race. If you should be unable to select such men from your patrons, let those who engage in the race pad.

MAY PARTY.

This attraction should be given in the Spring. Ladies should be dressed in white, and wear straw hats; gentlemen should also wear straw hats and light colored suits. Prizes should be given for the lady wearing the handsomest straw hat, and also for the handsomest dress.

BAND MARCH.

With four or five evenings' practice members of a band who can skate, will be able to play their instruments and skate at the same time. There is one band in the United States that makes a business of going over the country and giving "The Band March," charging one hundred dollars a night for their services. As before stated, with a little practice, any band can do as well.

The Main Street Rink band of sixteen pieces, of Richmond, Ind., with four nights' practice, were able to conduct the Grand March without any errors. The regular leader of the Grand March should lead the band. This attraction drew an immense house.

BARBER POLE.

Eight couples should participate. Ladies and gentlemen should be dressed as described in May Pole. The pole should be secured to the floor as the May Pole, and the same colored ribbon used and in the same arrangements. Have the Barber Pole just prior to the Grand March, which should be led by the couples that took part in the Barber Pole.

APPLE RACE.

Place several rows of apples parallel to each other, having the rows sufficiently wide apart so that the contestants will not interfere with each other, and place the apples about two feet apart, making the rows as long as the rink will admit. At the head of each row place a basket large enough to hold all the apples in the row. The contestants at a signal are to pick up the apple nearest the basket and put it in the basket, then skate to the next apple and put it in the basket, and so on. The contestant gathering all the apples up first in his row, getting one at a time and putting them in the basket, wins the race.

APRON CARNIVAL.

This attraction is for ladies only. White aprons with neat borders, and ladies wearing white caps, make a pretty sight. Induce ladies to decorate with real flowers as much as possible. Offer prizes for the prettiest apron. No lady should be permitted without wearing an apron.

WHEELBARROW ON SKATES.

This race should be between not more than two, and they should start from opposite parts of the hall.

FOOT BALL.

For this attraction choose sides just as when foot ball is played on foot. The game is to be played according to rules applying to foot ball. It will be well to remove any glass globes that may be on chandeliers before commencing the game, as there will be danger of breaking them.

POTATO RACE.

This race is contested in the same manner as the apple race, excepting that instead of picking up the potato with the hand it is to be picked up on the point of a sharp stick which each contestant should be furnished with. The stick should be about three feet long and the potato is to be carried on the point of the stick to the basket. In case the potato should drop off on the way to the basket, the contestant must stop and pick it up again with the stick as before, and carry it to the basket before proceeding to get the next potato.

Any one contestant will be allowed to knock the potato off of the stick of another by means of his own, and thus retard the opponent.

PRIZE NIGHT.

This attraction has the effect of charming every patron, at least before the drawing. For admission this night sell coupon tickets, the number on the ticket and coupon corresponding, detatching the coupon at the door. At about nine o'clock the drawing should take place, and in the following manner: Place all tickets in a hat and shake them up thoroughly. Blindfold a boy and let him take from the hat one ticket at a time and the number on the ticket be read aloud. Arrange so that the twentieth ticket be the winning one. if only one prize is given, and if there are to be two prizes, select the successful numbers, as twenty and thirty. A scal skin cap is a nice prize for a gentleman, and a toilet set for a lady.

BLIND RACE.

This race is interesting though of neccesity it must be slow. See that contestants are hoodwinked and all start from one starting place. Judges should be stationed about the track to warn the contestants in case of any danger and to see that they keep within the circle. The number of laps will depend upon the size of the rink.

——— —

MOTHER HUBBARD PARTY.

This party is for either ladies or gentlemen, or for ladies alone. The Manager can arrange for this as he sees fit. A prize should be given to the lady wearing the finest and prettiest Mother Hubbard.

——— —

BOYS' RACE.

This attraction is a drawing one for children as well as adults. There should be a series of three races, and have them occur every Saturday afternoon. Permit as many boys to enter the race as the size of the track will accomodate. Get a different lot of boys for each race, and at the close of the series let the last race be composed only of boys who have been winners in the preceding race. Use admission tickets to the Rink as prizes.

ST. VALENTINE'S DAY.

As this day in 1886 comes on Sunday, Saturday should be selected in place of it. Devote the afternoon to children, presenting each child with a valentine at the door. Fringed valentines that would be suitable for them can be bought at three dollars per hundred. In the evening require every body to wear a valentine that goes on the floor. In the evening sell the valentines at ten cents each. In this way a neat sum can be made off of them. Give prizes for persons wearing the most beautiful valentine and also a prize to the person wearing the most complete valentine costume.

CANDLE RACE.

Supply each contestant with a lighted candle in a candle-stick so that no grease will get on the floor, and also matches. The contestants are to start from a given point, and shall be obliged to carry the candle in an upright position and away from the body. If in the course of the race the light should become extinguished, the contestant must stop and light it before proceeding any further. The length of the race can be determined by the Manager.

CARNIVALS.

Masked Carnivals, Fancy Dress Carnivals, and Childrens' Masked Carnivals, for Saturday afternoon are not new as every Rink Manager knows, and we only call attention to them to suggest that it may be profitable to give such an attraction occasionally.

CHINESE LANTERNS IN A GRAND MARCH.

Provide each person that takes part in the March with a Chinese lantern. When all ready light all lanterns, and when this is done, turn down the lights just as low as possible. Care should be taken that one person does not run into another, as by such an accident the lanterns might be set on fire. The music during the March, and the lanterns in the darkness, make a very pleasing effect.

SLOW RACE.

This race is conducted like all other races. The contestants all start from the same place, and throughout the race are to keep moving forward all the time, the man coming in last to be declared the winner. Usually two laps will be enough for this race.

SPECTACLE CARNIVAL.

Every person on the floor should be obliged to wear glasses. We suggest that goggles, of various colored glass, be worn, nose glasses, dude glass for one eye, and anything in the shape of spectacles. A prize should be given to the person wearing the largest pair of glasses.

―――――

PENNY PICKING.

Secure at least twenty boys for this attraction. At the proper time clear the floor of all persons excepting the boys who are to take part in the "Picking." Collect all the boys in the center of the rink, and at a given signal throw a handful of pennies broad-cast on the floor, and when these are all gathered, throw another handful, and so on until four or five dollars have been thrown. For prizes let the boys keep all the pennies they can secure in the general scramble for them.

COUPLE CARNIVAL.

This night should be set apart exclusively for couples, and no lady without an escort or any gentleman without a lady should be permitted on the floor until after the Grand March. A prize should be given to the best and most graceful couple.

FAT MAN'S NIGHT.

This night should be well advertised as the Fat Man's Night. Induce all the fat men you know to come on the floor, and then as many persons as you can secure to pad. Give a prize to the really fattest man, and also one to the one best padded.

FAN CARNIVAL.

In this carnival every person on the floor shall be obliged to carry a fan. Give prizes for the largest, smallest, and handsomest fan.

CRACKER RACE.

Arrange contestants at starting point, giving each a cracker. At a given signal each contestant is to eat the cracker entirely; when this is done he is to skate once about the rink to the place of starting, when he is to eat another cracker entirely before starting, as before, and so on until five crackers have been eaten. The person eating five crackers shall be the winner.

CHILDREN'S WHITE DRESS CARNIVAL.

This carnival should be given on Saturday afternoon, so as not to interfere with their school duties. The rink should be darkened and lighted, as the effect will be much more beautiful. This carnival will be mostly for little girls, but there should be no objection to boys entering, and when they do, they should wear white waists. None but children should be allowed on the floor.

THE OBSTACLE RACE.

Suspend two solid, smooth barrels from the ceiling, by strong ropes, about fifty feet from the starting point, and hang the barrels at an angle of about forty-five degrees, so that the lower end of the barrel is about four feet from the floor. Immediately beyond the barrels place as many sawbucks and saws as there are contestants, and as many sticks of wood, of equal size, in front of the sawbucks on the floor; a little further on a greased teeter-totter about three feet wide; then one large barrel a little further on, suspended as the two already described. Then a little further on suspend three ladders from the ceiling with heavy ropes, then a little further as many step-ladders as there are contestants, and on the top of the ladder place a piece of hot wienerwurst thoroughly saturated with horseradish, the stronger the better.

The contestants start from a given point, where are placed as many chairs as there are contestants, with an apple on each chair. Skate around the rink to the chairs. Each contestant is to take the apple from the chair, sit down on the chair and eat the apple entirely before rising from the chair. When the apple is eaten, skate to the two suspended barrels, and go through either one of them from the lower end, then skate to one of the sawbucks, pick up the stick of wood, place it on the buck and saw the same in two. Unknown to the contestants, the blades should be taken from the saws and reversed. Then skate over the teetertotter, which should be greased, to the large barrel, and go through or over it; then skate to suspended ladders, and crawl through between the rounds; then skate to step-ladders, and go to top and sit on the top step, and eat the wienerwurst completely before coming down; then come down, and skate once around the rink to the place of beginning. The one getting there first wins the prize. It would be well to offer two prizes.

The step-ladders, sawbucks, teeter, and chairs should be placed just inside of the race circle, and men should hold the barrels and ladders back so as not to interfere with the contestants in making the first, and last lap around the rink. Judges should be placed at each obstacle to see that each contestant performs all duties required of him.

RED, WHITE, AND BLUE RIBBON.

All persons on the floor shall be required to wear ribbon in some shape, of either red, white, or blue color, or all. The ladies should decorate themselves with ribbon as their tastes incline, and the gentlemen should wear ribbon bows as button hole bouquets. Prizes should be given to the lady having the most artistic ribbon decoration, also the gentleman wearing the handsomest bow, and then to the person wearing the longest single ribbon.

CHICKEN HUNT.

Blindfold several boys, and then turn a chicken with clipped wings in the rink, first arranging so that the chicken can not get to the audience. The boy catching the chicken to win the prize.

BASE BALL.

Describe a diamond on the floor with chalk, making it as large as the rink will admit. Select two nines, and umpire and play according to the regular rules of the game as nearly as possible. A hollow rubber ball about the size of a base ball, and light pine bats should be used. In case the ball should be knocked among the audience, the umpire should call time until the ball is on the floor again. In advertising this attraction, assure patrons that there will be no danger.

Below we reprint an account of a game between the Rochesters and Binghamptons, New York:

BASE BALL ON ROLLER SKATES.

THE PEOPLE OF BINGHAMPTON WITNESS A GAME REPLETE
WITH LUDICROUS INCIDENTS.

[Special Correspondence of Rink and Roller.]

BINGHAMPTON, August 5. — The Pioneer Rink was filled to overflowing last night by one of the most fashionable assemblages ever held within its walls. The cause of the gathering was a contest at the national game between the members of the Rochester and Binghampton nines, in the State League. A regular diamond, with base, captain, players, and foul lines was laid out on the floor, and every requirement of the diamond field was had.

The two teams have played many exciting games on the field this season, but they have not previously played a game which afforded so much merriment to the lookers on, or fun for themselves. From start to finish the contest was exciting, and replete with ludicrous happenings. Few of the players had ever before enjoyed a trip on the little wheels, and they afforded many opportunities for general laughter, by their awkward endeavors to play ball and skate at the same time. As ball players they rank high, but as skaters they were failures; and it really was their lack of knowledge regarding the rollers that afforded so much sport.

On ordinary occasions the spectators at base ball games in this city are well behaved, and treat that much abused official, the umpire, with great consideration, but last night the crowd forgot itself. It actually broke out into one loud guffaw as Umpire Callaghan tried to skate and decide a play at second base. Under ordinary circumstances Mr. Callaghan would have made a correct decision. He would have gazed at the base runner, and yelled, "Yer out, yer out."

He did not do so last night.

Oh, no!

He looked toward second base and started toward it to obtain a better view of the play, and then failed to see it.

Soon after starting toward second base Mr. Callaghan became painfully aware that his feet were for the nonce beyond his control.   His north leg started eastward, and his south leg made a dash toward San Francisco.   His eyes involuntarily sought the maple floor.   Then Mr. Callaghan saw more stars than are in the constellation, and he forgot second base, the base runner, and even the axioms of base ball.   He blurted out, "Great scot."   The crowd laughed again.   When Mr. Callaghan arose and dusted off the bosom of his trousers the crowd roared heartily.

Thus were five innings played through.   More would have been played, but though it may seem paradoxical, the game would have to be called on account of daylight. Finally the Binghampton team won by a score of 3 runs to 0, and the crowd cheered enthusiastically for "the boys" and the umpire.

THE GOLD HUNT.

After securely blindfolding as many as shall participate in the hunt, suspend a five dollar gold piece from the ceiling by means of a string; then announce to the participants that the one who finds the money first shall keep it.   Before they start on the hunt the audience should be cautioned to make no remark, or in any way do anything that would tend to reveal the locality of the coin.

CHRISTMAS TREE ON CHRISTMAS NIGHT.

Place in the center of the rink as large an evergreen tree as is possible to get in the rink. Decorate it profusely with presents, selecting such as are generally inexpensive, and calculated to produce laughter. There should also be some presents of real value. Advertise that every patron will receive a present, and prepare accordingly. Attach to every article on the tree a number, and present for every admission ticket purchased a number corresponding with some number on the tree.

The tree should be arranged and decorated the day before, and covered with canvass until the time for gathering the presents, which should commence about half past nine, or ten o'clock, when all skating should be stopped. Any one who has participated in the festivities of a Christmas Tree will be assured of the success of this attraction.

CHILDREN'S CANDY MATINEE.

Select Saturday afternoon for this attraction. Present each child, at the door, with a package of candy. By purchasing candy at wholesale price a great many packages can be made at little expense.

These little attractions for children are always drawing, and result in large profit.

FLOWER CONTEST.

Blindfold the contestants, and then turn them around five or six times. When this has been done, suspend a basket of flowers from the ceiling to within about five feet of the floor, in any part of the rink that may seem proper. Caution everybody to keep still, and give no hints to the contestants as to the location of the basket. The contestant finding the basket shall be declared the winner, and receive the same as a prize. In case flowers can not be procured, a basket of fruit will do as well.

RINK BALL.

The rules of this roller skating game, which was successfully played eight years ago at the Clermont Avenue Rink, Brooklyn, N. Y., are such as to present the means of a very lively and exciting game, fully as much so as polo, without the chances for painful and frequently severe injuries that polo presents. What with the rather heavy ash sticks used in polo, and the wild efforts made to strike the ball in the midst of a rush of players to reach it, pretty hard knocks are interchanged. Then, too, the ball weighing seven ounces, is a dangerous one to be sent flying by a hard blow from the polo stick, as it frequently is. Rink ball is simply a modification of football, with the difference that the ball, instead of being kicked from goal to goal, is "dribbled" along the floor with the hands. It is a capital practice game for ballplayers, as it teaches them to bend for ground balls. As it was played in the old Brooklyn rink in 1876, these are the

RULES OF THE GAME.

1. Eleven players shall constitute a match

team, but the game may be played by as few as six on a side. When eleven on a side are played, they are placed as follows: Two to guard the goal, three in front of these as "backs," and the others further in front as rushers.

2. One umpire, selected by the two captains, shall decide all disputed points, and his decision shall be final.

3. The ball shall be a hollow rubber ball not to exceed four and a half ounces in weight, and to be not less than four and a half inches in diameter and fifteen inches in circumference.

4. The ball must not be kicked by any contestant, nor picked up from the floor, it only being in play when it is rolled or "dribbled" along the floor of the rink when being pushed or struck with the player's hand.

5. Any player *kicking* the ball during the progress of a game, or striking it with his hands so that it is lifted above the head of any other player, shall be at once declared out of play by the umpire, and he shall not take further part in the game until a touchdown be scored by either side.

6. The goal-line shall be a line marked on the

floor within ten feet from the boundary lines of the field, at each end thereof; and it shall be in length one-half the width of the rink-field, or of the width from one side boundary line to the other.

7. Outside the boundary lines is "out of touch," and when the ball goes outside either of the boundary lines it is dead until placed in play again by the umpire.

8. A "touchdown" shall be scored to the credit of the side whose player makes it, whenever the ball is fairly rolled, dribbled, or lifted across the goal-line of the opposing side, provided the ball is not lifted over the line higher than the heads of the fielders.

9. When the ball has been *kicked*—accidentally or otherwise—a "foul" shall be declared by the umpire, and the ball must be returned to the place from which it was thus unfairly removed. When the ball, too, is picked up by a fielder, or struck so that it be sent higher than the heads of the fielders, it shall be similarly declared foul, and returned to the place from which it was picked up or thrown.

10. Three touchdowns shall constitute a game, and the best two out of three games, or best three in five, constitute a match.

11. Should no touchdowns be scored within thirty minutes of the call of "play" by the umpire, the side first scoring a touchdown thereafter shall be credited with the game.

12. At the beginning of the game the umpire shall take the ball and place it in the center of the rink field, and when the captains of each side have placed their men in position, he shall call "play," and until such call is made the game can not begin.

13. When "time" is called by the umpire, play shall cease at once, and the ball shall be considered dead thereafter, until the umpire again calls "play."

14. Any match not decided in accordance with Rule 10, shall be regarded as drawn.

15. At no time during the progress of a match shall either the goal player or the backs be allowed to cross the center line of the rink-field in pursuit of the ball, except when called upon to take the place of a forward player.

DIAGRAM FOR TENNIS FIELD.

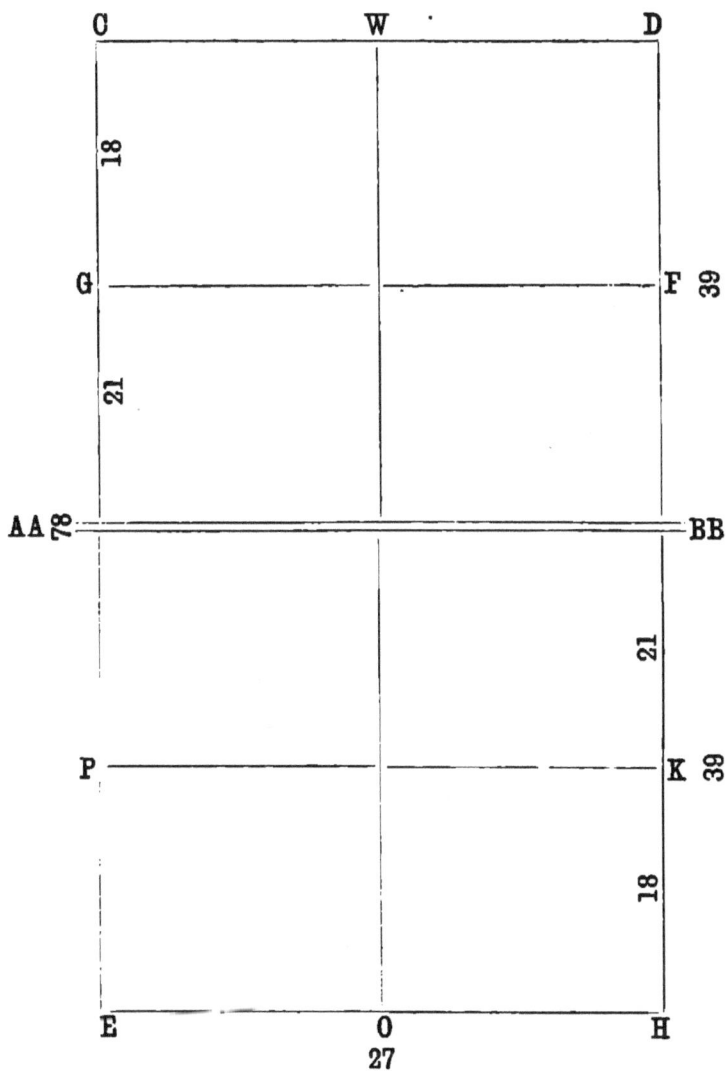

C   W   D

18

G   F 39

21

AA 78   BB

21

P   K 39

18

E   O   H

27

LAWN TENNIS ON ROLLER SKATES.

This fashionable game can be played in a rink with as much interest as on a lawn. The following description of the court and rules of the game will give full instructions.

LAWS OF LAWN TENNIS.

The Court.

1. The Court is 78 feet long and 27 feet wide. It is divided across the middle by a net, the ends of which are attached to two posts, AA

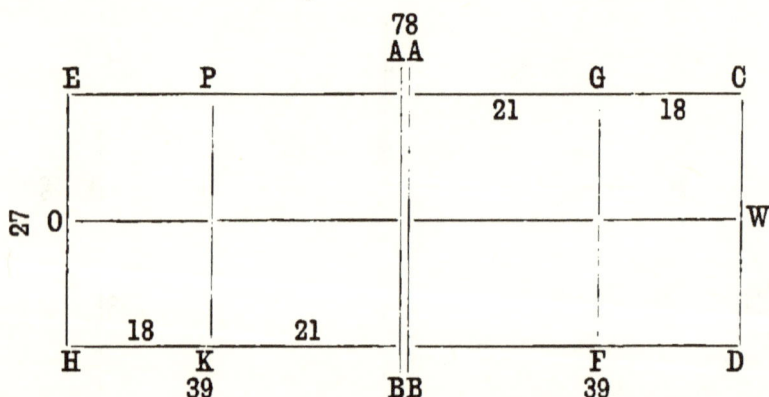

and BB, standing three feet outside of the court on either side. The height of the net is three feet outside of the court on either side. The height of the net is three feet six inches at the posts, and three feet in the middle. At each end of the court, parallel with the net, and 39 feet from it, are drawn the base lines C D and E H, the ends of which are connected by the side lines D H and C E. Half way down the side lines, and parallel with them is drawn the half-court line O W, dividing the space on each side of the net into two equal parts, the right and left courts. On each side of the net, at a distance of 21 feet from it, and parallel with it, are drawn the service lines G F and P K.

The Balls.

2. The Balls shall measure not less than $2\frac{15}{32}$ inches, nor more than $2\frac{1}{2}$ inches in diameter; and shall weigh not less than $1\frac{15}{16}$ oz., nor more than 2 oz.

The Game.

3. The choice of sides, and the right to serve in the first game shall be decided by toss; provided that, if the winner of the toss choose the right to serve, the other player shall have choice of sides, and vice versa. If one player choose the court, the other may elect not to serve.

4.   The players shall stand on opposite sides of the net; the player who first delivers the ball shall be called the server, and the other the striker-out.

5.   At the end of the first game the striker-out shall become server, and the server shall become striker-out; and so on alternately in all the subsequent games of the set, or series of sets.

6.   The Server shall serve with one foot on the base line, and with the other foot behind that line, but not necessarily upon the floor. He shall deliver the service from the right and left courts, alternately; beginning from the right.

7.   The ball served must drop between the service line, half court line, and side line of the court, diagonally opposite to that from which it was served.

8.   It is a Fault if the server fail to strike the ball, or if the ball served drop in the net, or beyond the service line, or out of court, or in the wrong court; or if the server do not stand as directed in Law 6.

9.   A ball falling on a line is regarded as falling in the court bounded by that line.

10.   A fault can not be taken.

11. After a fault the server shall serve again from the same court from which he served that fault, unless it was a fault because he served from the wrong court.

12. A fault can not be claimed after the next service is delivered.

13. The server shall not serve until the striker-out is ready. If the latter attempt to return the service he shall be deemed ready.

14. A service or fault delivered when the striker-out is not ready, counts for nothing.

15. The service shall not be volleyed, *i. e.*, taken, before it has touched the floor.

16. A ball is in play after leaving the server's racket, except as provided for in Law 8.

17. It is a good return, although the ball touch the net; but a service, otherwise good, which touches the net, shall count for nothing.

18. The server wins a stroke if the striker-out volley the service, or if he fail to return the service or the ball in play; or if he return the service or the ball in play so that it drops outside of his opponent's court; or if he otherwise loses a stroke as provided by Law 20.

19. The striker-out wins a stroke if the server serve two consecutive faults; or if he fail to return the ball in play; or if he return the ball in play so that it drops outside his opponent's court; or if he otherwise lose a stroke as provided by Law 20.

20. Either player loses a stroke if he return the service or the ball in play so that it touches a post of the net; or if the ball touch him or anything that he wears or carries, except his racket in the act of striking; or if he touch the ball with his racket more than once; or any of its supports while the ball is in play; or if he volley the ball before it has passed the net; or if the service or the ball in play touch a ball lying in his court.

21. In case any player is obstructed by any accident, the ball shall be considered a let.

22. On either player winning his first stroke, the score is called 15 for that player; on either player winning his second stroke, the score is called 30 for that player; on either player winning his third stroke, the game is called 40 for that player; and the fourth stroke won by either player, except as below: If both players have won three strokes, the play is called *deuce;* and the next

stroke won by either player is called *advantage* for that player.   If the same player wins the next stroke, he wins the game; if he loses the next stroke, the score returns to deuce; and so on until one player wins the two strokes immediately following the score of deuce, when game is scored for that player.

23.   The player who first wins six games, wins the set; except as below: If both players win five games, the score is called *games all;* and the next game won by either player is scored *advantage games* for that player.   If the same player wins the next game, he wins the set; if he loses the next game, the score returns to games all; and so on, until either player wins the two games immediately following the score of games all when he wins the set. Individual clubs at their own tournaments may modify this rule at their discretion.

24.   The players shall change sides at the end of every set; but the umpire, on appeal from either player, before the toss for choice, may direct the players to change sides, if, in his opinion, either side have a distinct advantage, owing to the sun, wind, or any other accidental cause; but if

the appeal be made after the toss for choice, the umpire may only direct the players to change sides at the end of every game of the odd or deciding set.

25.   When a series of sets are played, the player who served in the last game of one set shall be striker-out in the first game of the next.

26.   The Referee shall call the game after an interval of five minutes between sets, if either player so order.

27.   The above laws shall apply to the three-handed and four-handed games, except as modi-fied by rules on following pages.

THE THREE-HANDED AND FOUR-HANDED GAMES.

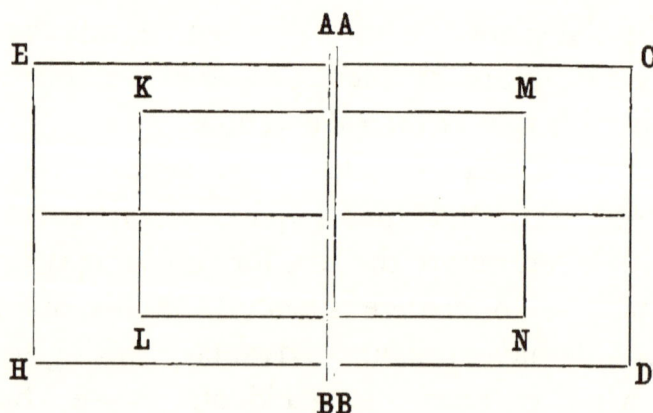

28. For the three-handed and four-handed games the court shall be 36 feet in width, 4½ feet inside the side lines, and parallel with them are drawn the service lines K M and L N. The service lines are not drawn beyond the point at which they meet the service side lines, as shown in the diagram.

29. In the three-handed game, the single player shall serve in every alternate game.

30. In the four-handed game, the pair who have the right to serve in the first game shall decide which partner shall do so; and the opposing pair shall decide in like manner for the second game. The partner of the player who served in the first game shall serve in the third, and the partner of the player who served in the second game shall serve in the fourth, aad the same order shall be maintained in all subsequent games of the set.

31. At the beginning of the next set, either partner of the pair which struck out in the last game of the last set may serve, the same privilege being given to their opponents in the second game of the new set.

32. The players shall take the service altern-

ately throughout the game; a player can not receive a service delivered to his partner; and the
order of service and striking out once established
shall not be altered, nor shall the striker-out change
courts to receive the service, till the end of the set.

33.   It is a fault if the ball served does not drop
between the service line, half-court line, and service side-line of the court, diagonally opposite to
that from which it was served.

34.   In matches the decision of the umpire shall
be final.   Should there be two umpires, they shall
divide the court between them, and the decision
of each shall be final in his share of the court.

ODDS.

35.   A Bisque is one point which can be taken
by the receiver of the odds at any time in the set,
except as follows:

(*a*)   A bisque can not be taken after a service is
delivered.

(*b*)   The server may not take a bisque after a
fault, but the striker-out may do so.

36.   One or more bisques may be given to in-
crease or diminish other odds.

37. Half fifteen is one stroke given at the beginning of the second, fourth, and every subsequent alternate game of a set.

38. Fifteen is one stroke given at the beginning of every game of a set.

39. Half thirty is one stroke given at the beginning of the first game, two strokes given at the beginning of the second game, and so on alternately in all subsequent games of the set.

40. Thirty is two strokes given at the beginning of every game of a set.

41. Half forty is two strokes given at the beginning of the first game, three strokes given at the beginning of the second game, and so on alternately, in all subsequent games of the set.

42. Forty is three strokes given at the beginning of every game of a set.

43. Half court: The players may agree into which half court, right or left, the giver of odds shall play; and the latter loses a stroke if the ball returned by him drop outside any of the lines which bound that half court.

RULES FOR UMPIRES.

1. There should be two umpires for each game,

unless there is a raised stand by the net.

2. If there are two umpires, they should be placed in the following manner: The umpire on the service side should stand opposite the end of the base line, so as to be able to see if the server stands as required. It is his duty to watch the base line and one side line throughout its entire length. The other umpire should stand opposite the service line on the other side until the service is returned, and should then fall back to the end of the base line diagonally opposite to the other umpire. He is to watch his base line, and the whole side line on his side. In the absence of a scorer the two umpires shall arrange which shall call the score.

3. It is the duty of the umpire to call faults, strokes, games and sets, when scored, or when requested to do so; not to call play, nor to give advice of any kind.

4. If, in his opinion, one side has a distinct advantage, and he is appealed to to direct the players to change sides at the end of every game, he has no option whatever, but must direct them to do so, and remind them at the end of each game.

5. In the four-handed games there should be a third umpire at the net, whose only duty is to see that the rules regarding the net are observed. He usually, however, also acts as referee.

POLO.

Polo specially commends itself as an attraction for rinks and skaters. When governed by proper rules and regulations the game becomes very scientific, requiring skill in skating and good judgment.

A general idea of the game can be obtained by reading the rules. The players are divided equally, each club having substitutes to be ready in case of accident. Each club has a goal to defend and attack. The starting point is usually the center of the field or rink; the object of the game being to knock the ball with the *polo sticks* through the goal of the opposing club. The tactics pursued in football are most likely to ensure success in Polo; a gentle, nursing hit, keeping the ball well in hand, and when hard pressed by the opposing side, passing it to another of one's own side, not endeavoring to rush the goal without a fair chance of securing it. The ball should at no time be raised from the skating surface. The field should be rectangular. The size of the rectangle will depend upon the size of the rink.

SPALDING'S POLO RULES.

[Published by permission of Messrs. A. G. SPALDING & BRO., of Chicago and New York.]

RULE 1. Each team shall consist of seven players, to be distinguished as follows: One goal tend; two half-backs; one cover point; two rushers.

RULE 2. The ball shall be the Spalding Regulation Polo Ball. The sticks shall not exceed four feet in length or one inch in diameter, and shall not exceed sixteen ounces in weight.

RULE 3. The goals shall be composed of two upright posts, three feet high, and not more than two inches in diameter, set in blocks not over ten inches square and two inches thick. They shall be placed in line $4\frac{1}{2}$ feet apart, measuring from the posts, and not less than six feet from the end of the surface.

RULE 4. Only one person shall tend goal at a time.

RULE 5. There shall be a referee, chosen by the captains, two judges for each side, and a time-keeper. A judge from each side shall stand behind each goal. No persons but the players, referee and judges shall be permitted on the surface during a match, unless assistance is to be rendered in case of an accident, or unless upon mutual invitation of the captains and referee. The referee shall start and call the game, and settle all disputed points. The judges at each goal shall determine when a goal is won, except in case of a disagreement between them, and then the referee may determine the matter.

RULE 6. The referee shall toss for the position of the teams in presence of the captains.

RULE 7. To start the game, the ball shall be placed at the middle of a straight line drawn through the center of each goal, and at the whistle of the referee shall be charged upon by a player from each team.

RULE 8. To constitute a match three out of five goals must be won by one of the competing teams, unless a different agreement be made by the captains, in presence of the referee, previous to the beginning of the match. Unless a goal be won meantime the referee shall call game at the end of each half hour. If three out of five goals be the game played, if at the final call of game by the referee one team shall have won two goals to none for the other, the winners of the two goals shall be considered winners of the match. If there be a postponement by the referee, the match shall be renewed where it terminated; but the *personnel* of each team must be the same.

RULE 9. A goal is won by the passsage of the ball, from the front, between the goal posts below the top of the same. If by accident one or both of the goal posts should be knocked over, and it is apparent that the ball passed through the proper bounds, it shall be a goal.

RULE 10. If the ball go out of bounds the referee shall blow his whistle to call game, and place the ball at the point opposite where it went out, at least four feet from the rail. In recommencing play, the players who do so must stand in position to knock the ball lengthwise of the surface, with their backs toward the sides.

RULE 11. Game should be called by the referee whenever a foul occurs, or whenever one is claimed, unless the referee is satisfied, by his own observation at the moment, that no just claim exists. Upon a claim of foul, if game is to be renewed, the ball must be placed where the foul occurred.

RULE 12. It shall be deemed a foul: 1—if any player stop or strike the ball when any part of his person is touching the surface; 2—if any player catch or bat the ball with his hands or arms; 3— if any player, save the goal tend, who may do so, kick the ball with his foot or skate, though he may stop the ball with either.

RULE 13. Any act by any player that is manifestly intended as an unwarrantable intererence by one player with another may be declared a foul by the referee, upon complaint by the captain of the offended side.

RULE 14. Three fouls, other than when the ball leaves the bounds, made by either side during a contest for a goal, shall constitute a goal for the opposing side.

RULE 15. If the referee decide that a foul by the goal tend prevented a goal from being made, it shall be adjudged as a goal for the opposite side.

RULE 16. If any club refuse to abide by the decision of the referee, which, in all cases, shall be final, the game shall be declared forfeited to the opposing club.

RULE 17. In case of any injury to any player a substitute may be appointed.

* * *

RINK RULES.

The following rules were arranged for one of the largest rinks in the country. It would be well to have a number of them printed on card-board and placed in conspicuous places in the rink.

1. Skating begins at one stroke of the gong, and ceases at two strokes of the gong.

2. No smoking allowed in or about the premises, except in the smoking room.

3. Gentlemen will not soil the floor with tobacco; others will not be permitted to do so.

4. Crowding, loud talking or other rude or noisy demonstrations, are forbidden.

5. No one should stand, even for a moment, on the skating surface, or so as to obstruct the entrance to the place, or the view of others.

6. In putting on skates, see that that the buckles are upon the outside of the foot.

7. Never cross the skating surface in passing to or from a seat; always follow the direction of the skaters.

8. Spitting or throwing any substance upon the skating surface is dangerous, and will not be permitted.

9. Going up or down stairs with skates on is dangerous and strictly prohibited.

10. No stick, cane, string, or other similar article, should be taken on the floor.

11. In skating around the circuit, all will observe a uniform direction, taking great care never to interfere with the movements of others.

12. No skater should stop, even for an instant, in the circuit, except to assist a lady.

13. Pushing, tripping, racing, tagging or taking hold of others' garments, or any rude or dangerous actions, are strictly forbidden.

14. Most falls occur from the feet being parallel

with each other, or nearly so, as in this position one foot can not check the movement of the other; hence, before attempting to stand upon the skates, the beginner should place the heels together, with the feet at right angles, in which position they should always be, while getting up, sitting down, or standing upon skates.

15. Skating by four, or more than two together, should be avoided, while skating in couples should be practiced as much as possible, by all sufficiently advanced, as there is no other way in which a lady and gentleman can make so graceful an appearance.

16. On removing the skates please return them to the skate room, with the heel strap of one skate buckled and tucked firmly into the buckle of the other skate to prevent mismating.

17. A cheerful compliance with the above, and a careful regard for the comfort and enjoyment of others, is respectfully requested.

18. None but those known, or supposed by the management to be acceptable to a majority of the patrons, will be admitted and furnished with skates.